Better Table Tennis

Better Table Tennis

by

Johnny Leach, M.B.E.

Officially approved by the
English Table Tennis Association

Kaye & Ward Ltd · London

First published by
Kaye & Ward Limited
194-200 Bishopsgate, London EC2
1969

© 1969 Kaye & Ward Limited

SBN 7182 0152 3

Printed in England by
Fletcher & Son Ltd, Norwich

Contents

Illustrations

The main demonstrators shown in the following
photographs are two English teenagers of
exceptionally high standard—Jill Shirley, of Bucks,
and Peter Taylor, of Herts. Peter's elder brother
Trevor, a left-hander, who like Jill Shirley, ranked
as England's No. 1 Junior at the time, is also featured.

The photographs were taken by Peter Madge.

The author, Johnny Leach, M.B.E.

MAKING A START

From the coach's point of view, the ideal beginner would be one who arrived for his first lesson without ever having held a bat in his hand. It is doubtful if such a person exists.

Ours is a 'fun' game for the home, as well as a major international sport when played more seriously, so nearly everyone has played table tennis in some shape or form before deciding to put himself in the hands of a coach.

So the coach's first task is usually to iron out bad habits and wrong ideas acquired through play in cramped, or otherwise unsuitable, conditions.

Like most, I imagine, I began playing on the dining room table at home. Fortunately for me my father knew something about the game so, in the first instance, he lowered the net in proportion to the size of the table.

As you probably know, the full-sized table common to all ages and standards is 9 feet long, 5 feet wide, standing 2 foot 6 inches above the floor. The height of the net should be 6 inches above the playing surface.

If the table you use at home is only 8 feet long you should lower the net to 5 inches, and so on, in proportion; otherwise you will be obliged to spoon the ball high most of the time, simply to get it over the net, so acquiring the habit of poor stroke production.

Another difficulty generally encountered is lack of space necessary to play proper strokes. How often has the close proximity of a sideboard led to a stubborn weakness in certain strokes! Admittedly, in some rare cases poor facilities have led to the invention of match-winning new strokes, but, despite this, to exercise one's ingenuity and effort simply to overcome unnecessary handicaps is scarcely a course to be recommended.

Ideally, the sooner you can transfer your attention to the *real* game on a full-sized table the better. Ours is a sport suitable for the whole family, and often it proves possible to equip the garage, attic, or large spare room at home in fully approved fashion. If not, for home play I would

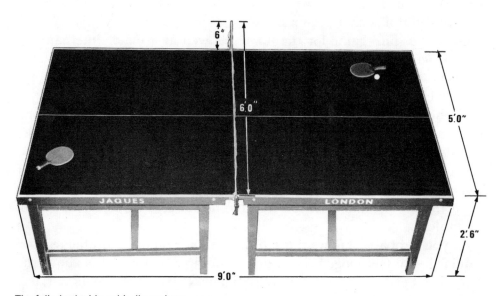

The full-sized table, with dimensions.

recommend the use of those plastic foam-covered bats specially designed to deaden the ball's speed on impact and so permit the use of full-blooded, correct strokes over a low net on a miniature table. Such equipment is generally available through sports shops. The type I myself would recommend is 'MINI-PING'.

AT WHAT AGE SHOULD YOU START?

Any age is the right age to start playing table tennis. I have stood a 5 year-old on a box, so enabling him to see and reach over the top of a full-sized table, and watched him play some quite lengthy rallies. I've also coached over-eighties! But the 1968 ladies singles' champion of Europe was a 14 year-old schoolgirl, so obviously, if international fame is your aim, the sooner you start the better.

A 'Mini-ping' match in progress; the real thing on a miniature scale.

I suppose the majority today start playing fairly seriously at ten, progressing through tournaments, school, club, county or state, and junior international team play to the senior ranks. There the ladder starts again right up to the pinnacle of the world championship.

11

A peak standard is usually reached in the early twenties, which can be maintained through growing experience often for several years; but once again there is no rule about this, and many older and younger players have emerged to upset all theories.

In case you are worried that your ability may not be noticed, let me assure you that table tennis is so well organised throughout the world today that it is virtually impossible for any player of genuine talent to escape recognition. Opportunities abound all the way up to the top—the only question is, are you sufficiently dedicated to grasp them to the exclusion of almost every other interest? If not, you must settle for the next-best-thing—finding your own level and enjoying competition against players of a similar standard. That, too, can be very rewarding; and, even then, the more study and practice you are prepared to put in, the more you will improve, the better your results will be and the more enjoyment you will get in the process.

CHANGES

Few sports have changed so dramatically in their first fifty years as table tennis. It is different from when I was a boy, largely because the bat surface in use today permits more varied strokes and greater speed and spin, but also because everything improves as we cash in on experience, and make ourselves fitter, faster and more competitive.

Bats were standardised in 1959, giving a choice of three different rubber surfaces, since when the use of the 'sandwich' bat has become virtually universal. During the next decade the speed of play reached a new height which is unlikely to be surpassed, at least while present equipment remains obligatory. But the game will continue to improve through greater consistency, still greater variation of strokes and hence more complex tactics.

In recent times there has also been a marked change in the coaching of the game. Once it was our aim to point pupils towards the ideal of performing every stroke fluently, each to the perfect pattern. Imagine our dismay when the Asians arrived on the world scene with their supposedly old-fashioned grips, and one-shot attacking style of play, to knock spots off the most graceful of our textbook exponents.

This made us realise several things: there is no such thing as 'ideal style'. Champions come in all shapes and sizes, often with vastly unorthodox styles and techniques. The modern game is so fast that the younger and fitter a player is, the better his or her chance of success. You must never stifle natural ability, but encourage it to develop in the way it wants to go. Being 'different' can give a big advantage.

Of course, the basic principles of correct stroke production still apply, but we adapt them to suit the individual—not the other way round, you note. A stroke is correct if it works consistently well.

We try to give each pupil a grounding in every stroke, without wasting his time needlessly on improving those which look wrong, providing he has found his own adequate compromise. At the same time we encourage him to concentrate on his own, natural, point-winning strokes in order to develop them. We take short cuts, because champions are getting younger all the time and their challengers must be brought to a still earlier peak.

Having said this, however, I don't want to give you the notion that table tennis today is right back to square one with experience counting for nothing.

On the contrary, no one ever became a champion without having a thorough knowledge of all the laws, the strokes and their counters, and how to fit technique into an effective tactical pattern. All these things you can learn from this book and practice on your own to reach a good standard. But you still wouldn't be a champion, or even a reasonably competent match-player without lots and lots of competitive experience, preferably with some first-hand help from an experienced coach along the way.

DRESS

Dark clothes are the general rule, to provide a background against which the white ball can be clearly seen. In the U.S.A. however, white clothing is allowed. This apart, neatness, and a comfortable fit to permit athletic movements, are the main considerations to govern one's choice.

A simple dark shirt and shorts for boys, a skirt or divided skirt for girls, with a good pair of rubber shoes—that's the fashion. A matching jersey, pullover or track suit to keep you warm between matches, or during early play, is a useful addition. Note that if this does *not* match your shirt in colour, and is worn in play, you may not discard it until the game has been completed.

Make sure your shoes have non-slip soles.

GROWING PAINS

It is quite common for a youngster who looked a potential champion at the age of ten or eleven to strike a patch where everything he tries seems to go wrong. At this point he may worry so much about his loss of touch that he loses interest altogether and takes up something else. That's a pity, because nearly always his failing ability can be attributed to the most natural of causes—he is growing up.

As one's height increases, and consequently one's relationship to a table of standard height, it is necessary to adjust the timing of one's strokes to suit. That's obvious, and not at all difficult to put right once you realise what your trouble is. This is one of those many occasions on which a little help from someone else can save weeks of fruitless effort and frustration.

From time to time a boy will come to me with the sorry tale that 'Just lately I cannot avoid hitting the ball off the table edge'. Wise lad for asking advice—far too many think it's just a case of their luck being out. Whenever faults develop there is a root cause. In this case, obviously, his timing has gone wrong. All he needs is someone to watch him in action for a while to determine whether he is hitting the ball too early, or too late.

To cure this he must either adjust the way in which he is producing his stroke, or the timing of its execution so the ball is hit before, or after it has reached its peak height.

Moral—don't be too proud to ask a more experienced player to watch you in action and say where he thinks you are going wrong. Often he can spot the trouble, and tell you how to cure it in a flash.

CHOICE OF BAT

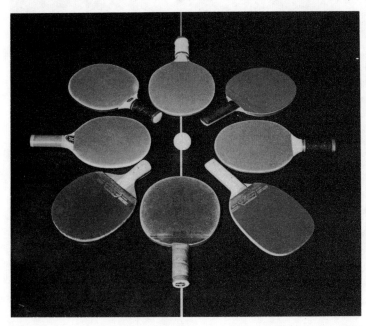

Selection of modern bats of all shapes and sizes. *Bottom centre* is my personal choice. To the *left* of this is the one-sided sandwich penhold bat favoured by the Chinese champions, and to the *right* is pictured the Japanese equivalent.

Though a table tennis bat may be of any size, shape or weight, one's choice of covering material on the wooden blade is restricted to the following types;

15

(1) plain, ordinary pimpled rubber, with pimples outward,

(2) sandwich, consisting of a layer of cellular rubber (known as 'sponge') surfaced by plain ordinary pimpled rubber as in (1)

(3) as in (2) but with pimples inward,

(4) a combination of any of the above surfaces.

(NOTE: the colour of the rubber on the two sides must be similar.)

The thickness of (1) must not exceed 2 millimetres and of (2) 4 millimetres.

Which bat should you choose?

As regards weight, one which feels just right and which you can handle with easy confidence. As regards surface, plain pimpled rubber facilitates

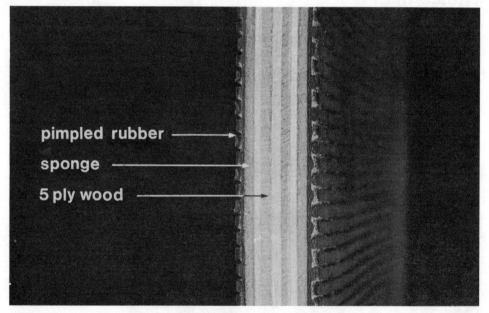

Section of a sandwich bat with pimples 'outward', i.e. Type (2), showing alternate layers of plywood, sponge and pimpled rubber.

good ball control and the acquisition of good all-round stroke play, but hardly anyone uses it in competitive play today. Nearly everyone uses (2), (3) or (4), the bats with the layer of sponge between the wood and the pimples, which has more 'give' to accentuate speed and spin. These may be a little harder for the beginner to master, but experience shows it is better to learn the most modern technique from the start. *In this book I shall treat sandwich as orthodox equipment, and deal with the production of strokes accordingly.*

It may be, of course, that you just can't get along with sandwich, in which case pimpled rubber would still be good enough to take you all the way to the world championship with the added, and growing advantage that many modern players are unused to opposing it, and so tend to regard this weapon, once nearly universal, as a freak.

As you advance you may wish to experiment. Generally, bat (2), with

The penhold grip of China's world champion Chuang Tse-Tung.

Showing how Chuang's fingers are placed behind the bat.

pimples outward, is used for more speed with spin, while (3), with pimples inward, is slower but gives extra spin.

Then again, several modern players find they get an advantage by using a combination of the permitted surfaces: for example, plain pimples on the side of the blade used for backhand strokes, sandwich on the side used for forehand.

17

Finally, we have the extra-light type of bat used by the Asian champions with their penhold grip. This has sandwich rubber on the business side, and nothing but wood on the other which is not used. If you find that you have a natural ability for 'Asian-style', I would be the last person to want to discourage you: on the contrary, as a good penhold player in the Western world you would be welcomed as a rare and challenging opponent.

Each type of bat requires a different technique, at least an adjustment in timing for every stroke. I will try to signpost the differences as we go along, but it is mostly a case of you finding the right timing, by trial and error, until it becomes instinctive.

Finally, take note that while the sandwich bat can lend your game some degree of artificial aid (as opposed to plain wood, or even plain, pimpled rubber) it will not make up for any deficiencies in your play— quite the contrary. *Remember: The player is more important than the bat.*

GRIP

Put your bat on the table, pick it up by its blade with your non-playing hand, then grasp the handle with your playing hand as if shaking hands with it. Does that grip come naturally, and feel right? It does to most Westerners, and is the basis of the one we use.

For forehand strokes the forefinger normally lies across the back of the blade to give more steadiness and better touch. The thumb is tucked out of the way, leaving three fingers curled round the handle.

When it comes to backhand strokes, most players reverse the positions of thumb and forefinger. The thumb moves up so it lies down the centre of the blade to give support, while the forefinger drops down near to the edge of the blade to avoid coming into contact with the ball on impact.

Many modifications are possible. For example some players like to have two fingers behind the blade for forehand strokes. This is perfectly in order. In fact almost anything goes, so long as you feel comfortable in playing your shots.

Try the orthodox grip first, then modify it to suit yourself.

The basic 'shake hands' grip (back view).

(front view).

Western grip, forehand variation (back view).

(front view).

STANCE

Using the 'shake hands'-type grip, ideally one should play nearly every stroke from a sideways stance, as illustrated in most of the photographs in this book.

19

For example, as a right-handed player, striking the ball on your forehand, you are best placed to perform a perfect stroke if you start with left shoulder and left leg nearer the table. For a backhand stroke it is your right shoulder and leg which should be nearer the table.

Jill demonstrates the ideal 'ready position' which is central, facing the table, feet about 18 in. apart, knees relaxed. From this position one can quickly cover a return made to any part of the table. For example . . .

one step forward to play a short ball on the forehand or

I advise you to learn the strokes by taking up the correct sideways stance, even though later on, when you start playing competitively, you may find it essential to modify this to cope with the greatly increased speed of play.

Many young players today have found it possible to play their shots, backhand or forehand, from what appears to be a square-on, rather than a sideways stance, hardly seeming to move to one side or the other. Watch them carefully, though, and you will see that, while they do not

backhand . . .

one step backward with the right foot, and a turn on the left heel to receive a deep fast shot on the forehand or . . .

get into the *full* sideways-on position, they do take up a semi-sideways stance by pivoting from the hips at the very last moment. This at least ensures getting a free swing at the ball without the body getting in the way.

21

If you find that you can play this way, (which involves using much less than the recommended amount of backswing, and body assistance which adds power to strokes) by all means do so. But every liberty taken with a basic principle demands compensation of some kind, so if

one pace backward with the left foot to deal similarly on the backhand wing.

you do shorten your backswing make sure that your stroke has the best possible chance of success *by extending your follow through to the maximum.*

The modified stances, which in turn call for modified stroke production, are important developments you will wish to study at a more advanced stage. Meantime, when learning I still think it best for you to learn to play the basic strokes from the full sideways-on stance, which can be reduced gradually to a necessary minimum as the speed of exchanges in your competitive matches start to demand special measures.

Another modern approach is to take up one's position on the extreme

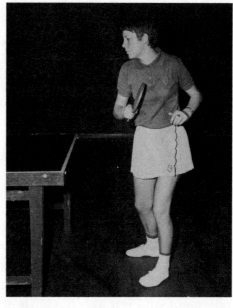

TOP LEFT:
Peter shows the quick swivel of the hips from square-on stance to adopt semi-sideways position for forehand play.

TOP RIGHT:
Jill shows the equivalent 'swivel' movement for backhand play.

BOTTOM LEFT:
Peter shows the position taken up by the strong forehand attacker, ready on the extreme backhand wing to cover the entire table with a forehand stroke.

backhand wing. This is favoured by the type of player whose greatest strength is forehand attack, which he is able to launch from any part of the court and wants to get going without delay. Before adopting this stance it is important to realise the risk involved. While it is quite possible to get across in time to respond aggressively to a service directed down the extreme forehand wing, an opponent's subsequent rapid switch of the ball, to the extreme backhand side, may leave you hopelessly stranded.

This could happen quite often, forcing you to take up a more orthodox position. Make sure you are equipped to do so, and to seek opportunities to get your forehand going from there.

PUSH STROKES

The simple 'push' is the 'marking time' stroke in match play. It can be used at any time with safety, against almost any stroke employed by an opponent, and it is also the basis of nearly all the other strokes.

Peter's Forehand Push—Approach.

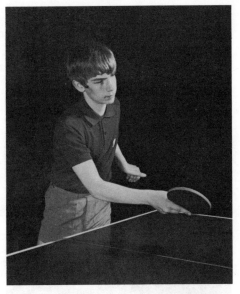

Peter's Forehand Push—Contact

Peter's Forehand Push—Follow-through.

As its name implies it means merely pushing the ball back across the net, using either forehand or backhand, but in such a way that you are not merely setting yourself up for your opponent's 'kill'.

To learn to play the stroke correctly, it is best to start in the sideways stance so that your body will not impede your stroke. Forearm should be horizontal, and bat tilted slightly back at the top. Experience will show you how the angle of your bat must be altered to suit the type of spin imparted by your opponent, and to what extent. As a general guide, however, if returning a straightforward push with another push the tilt need be only slight, but a more exaggerated tilt is required to deal with a shot that has been heavily undercut, or given backspin (of which more anon).

Move the bat steadily forward and downward, at the same time transferring the weight of your body from the back to the front foot. Using a sandwich bat it is necessary on contact to give the ball a slight but definite 'lift' over the net, so your follow-through will be on a slightly upward plane. Don't neglect that follow-through, allowing your movements to continue naturally to their full extent after the ball has departed. This is very important. By continuing the movement of the

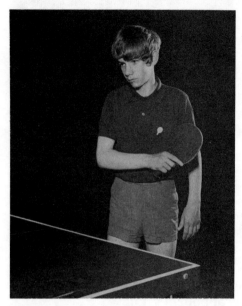

Peter's Backhand Push—Approach.   Peter's Backhand Push—Contact.

arm and the bat in the follow through you are keeping the bat in contact with the ball for the maximum possible time, so aiding control and accuracy.

Contact is usually made when the ball is level with your body, but may be delayed if the ball is approaching at speed. To return a short ball you must, of course, reach forward.

When making this stroke your control should be so complete that you can almost 'feel' the ball on your bat and so direct it to advantage over to the other side.

All that I have said applies equally to forehand or backhand. Practice playing push strokes from either wing alternately—it's a good way to get used to moving the feet rapidly into the appropriate sideways-on position for forehand or backhand. The feet keep the body balanced correctly, and a good balance is another vital factor in achieving good ball control.

Peter's Backhand Push—Follow-through.

Jill demonstrates the Push Shot using an ordinary pimpled rubber bat. This is the follow-through for the forehand shot—note that it is more on an even plane than the same stroke made with sandwich bat (see page 25 for comparison).

SPIN

Before seeing how the Push Stroke can lead us into other, more exciting strokes used in the game, it is important to get a grasp of the three basic spins used in table tennis. These are backspin, topspin and sidespin. The latter has come much more into the game in recent years because the sandwich bat has made it so much more reliable and effective.

Backspin makes the ball rotate backwards while it is moving forward. This spin is imparted by chopping the bat downwards behind and underneath the ball at the moment of striking it. The further underneath

As last picture, *backhand* (compare with Peter's follow-through on page 27).

the ball that the bat strikes, the greater the amount of backspin. Its effect is to give the ball a tendency to bounce backwards towards the striker after it has hit the table surface.

Topspin is the opposite, and the main counter to backspin. It makes the ball rotate forwards while it is moving forward. It is produced by brushing the bat upwards and forwards across the top of the ball as it is struck. Its effect is to give the ball a tendency to dip in flight over the net, and to shoot forward and upward on touching the table surface and before dipping again.

Sidespin makes the ball spin horizontally either to the left or right, and it is produced by moving the bat across the ball from one side to the other as it is struck. If struck from right to left, the ball will tend to break to your opponent's left-hand side after touching the table surface.

Sidespin is often used in conjunction with one of the other two basic spins, in which form it can be most effective.

When the square-on stance is employed, with its last moment pivot to play either backhand or forehand from the modified sideways position,

TOPSPIN BACKSPIN

direction of spin

direction of travel

Diagram: ball arrowed to show direction of Topspin.

direction of spin

direction of travel

Diagram: ball arrowed to show direction of Backspin.

the bat will tend to be drawn across the ball in playing a stroke. The result is, a certain amount of sidespin will naturally be imparted *in addition to whatever spin you deliberately impart.*

Should you also decide to add deliberate sidespin, some quite spectacular 'breaks' (on your opponent's side of the table) can be achieved.

The wrist can be used to bring the bat across the ball while playing a simple push stroke, and by breaking the wrist only at the very last moment the direction of your shot may be effectively disguised.

One word of warning here—too much use of the wrist promotes inconsistency. There is such little margin for error in timing.

Peter shows the follow through to a Forehand Push shot to which he has added sidespin— note that his bat has travelled forward and *across*.

Peter's approach to a Backhand Push Shot, to which he intends to add sidespin.

Follow-through to the above Backhand Push with Sidespin.

SERVICE

At one time Service was regarded merely as a means of introducing the ball into play. It now assumes much greater importance. With thought, and practice, you can develop a whole range of different services which, suitably varied and disguised can give you instant supremacy in a rally,

TOP LEFT:

Service. Ball resting correctly on the palm of her free hand, Jill prepares to make a Forehand Chop Service.

TOP RIGHT:

Forehand Chop Service—just before contact, which must be made *after* the ball starts to drop.

BOTTOM LEFT:

Forehand Chop Service—the follow-through

31

or even on occasions enable you to score a point outright. However, the first thing to do is to study the service law and ensure that you do not forfeit points yourself by serving incorrectly.

Service must always be made from the palm of the free hand, which must be open, fingers together and thumb free, stationary, and above the level of the playing surface. The ball should rest on the palm without being cupped or pinched in any way by the fingers.

Toss the ball up into the air from the palm, without spin, and as near vertically upwards as possible. The ball must be visible at all times to the

Jill's Backhand Chop service—moment of contact.

Jill's Backhand Chop service—follow-through.

Umpire, who will call a 'fault' if the ball should veer more than 45 degrees to either side of the vertical.

The ball must not be struck with the bat until it has started to descend from the peak of its trajectory. When struck it must first touch your own side of the table and then, passing directly over or around the net, touch the receiver's court.

32

Within those requirements there are four basic services to master, all of which can be varied by spin, speed, angling and placing. All are best made from the appropriate sideways stance.

Backspin Service can be made from either forehand or backhand, using the appropriate sideways stance. Hold the bat at near shoulder-height, the blade tilted forward at the bottom. As you throw up the ball with your free hand, bring the bat forward and downward to strike the ball just below its centre after it has dropped. Follow-through in a forward and slightly upward direction.

Jill's Forehand Topspin service—just after contact.

Jill's Forehand Topspin service—high follow-through.

Topspin Service (forehand or backhand). Leaning slightly forward, hold the bat just behind and below the ball, blade tilted forward. Throw up the ball from the free hand, then start to move the bat forward and upward. The idea is to brush the top of the ball when it has dropped to just above table level.

With each of these services, *think* before you put the ball into play.

Jill's Backhand Topspin Service—contact.

Jill's Backhand Topspin service—follow-through

Peter's Forehand Chop service *with sidespin*—approach.

34

TOP LEFT:

Peter's Forehand Chop service *with sidespin*— follow-through.

EXAMPLES OF COMMON SERVICE FAULTS— *to be avoided.*

BOTTOM LEFT:

Jill's hand, on which the ball rests, is being held below table level.

BOTTOM RIGHT:

Left-handed Trevor Taylor is concealing the ball from the umpire (seated on Trevor's right side).

MORE COMMON SERVICE FAULTS

TOP LEFT:

Jill is committing 2 faults here: she struck the ball while it was still on its upwards trajectory; and in striking the ball her bat is over the edge of the table.

TOP RIGHT:

This picture shows that Jill is cupping the ball in her free hand—again, this is not allowed.

BOTTOM LEFT:

Jill's Forehand Chop—Approach.

Are you completely settled and composed? Is your opponent ready? Are you clear where you are trying to place the ball, and what precise effect you are aiming to achieve?

Advantage can be gained by variation of speed and spin, placing and angling of the service. Also at an advanced level and with practice, you will find that you can combine sidespin with either topspin or backspin sometimes to score an 'ace', but the average player will find ample scope for variation in just the four basic services I have described.

DEFENSIVE STROKES

With the aid of the sandwich bat, you can return almost any ball within reach, simply by interceding your bat in the path of your opponent's shot.

Jill's Forehand Chop—
Contact.

Of course a deliberate stroke is more effective when time allows, but not essential because the sponge content in your bat covering will 'give'

slightly on impact, then at once spring back to boost the normal speed at which the ball would rebound.

The basic defensive stroke is the Chop, used from either forehand or backhand, which uses backspin to slow down an opponent's attack and frequently sets him problems of judgement as well.

Once again the sideways approach to this shot is the ideal, and the nearer you can get to assuming it in match-play the more powerful and effective your stroke is likely to be. You start with your weight on the back foot and transfer it to the front foot as your bat contacts the ball.

Approach the ball with your bat shoulder high, bending knees and trunk as your arm starts to move in a forward and downward path. Point of contact with the ball is behind, and below its centre, and it is best made when the ball is dropping and has reached waist height. Having chopped the ball with this forward and downward action, let the bat follow through in an upward curve so that it finishes just below

Jill's Backhand Chop—Approach.

Jill's Backhand Chop—Contact.

Jill's Backhand Chop—
Follow-through.

Jill demonstrates the follow-through for a Forehand Chop stroke made with an ordinary pimpled rubber bat—it is in a more upward direction.

shoulder-height. Try to get as much length with your shot as possible, taking care not to overshoot the table edge.

Backhand and forehand shots are made in a similar manner, but with foot positions changing appropriately. For a well controlled backhand chop, the full sideways stance is especially beneficial.

A quick switch from full forehand to full backhand stance must be made by jumping. Time does not allow for each foot to be moved separately.

As opposite, Backhand Chop.

Chop at close range—Jill's Forehand Approach.

Chop at close range—Jill's follow-through extends below table level.

Backhand Chop at close range—approach.

Backhand Chop at close range—follow-through

Jill demonstrates the Forehand Chop with added sidespin.

As above, the Backhand Chop with Sidespin. Note how Jill's bat comes across the front of her body.

On either wing aim to get into position as near behind the line of the ball as possible, since reaching upsets both balance and control. However, when in action you will be forced to compromise on several matters such as the precise point of contact, transference of body weight, positioning, and so on. Also the angle of your bat must alter to suit the type of shot you are dealing with—for example, it must sometimes be nearly horizontal to counter a very hard hit, when it may also be necessary to incorporate a turn of the wrist under the ball, as contact is made.

My advice is to learn the stroke under ideal conditions and to get as close as possible to the ideal when using it 'for real'.

THE FLOAT

The Float is a 'dummy chop', a deceptive stroke used mostly by defensive players which, if not recognised for what it is and played as normal backspin, forces the receiver to lift his return off the end of the table.

The normal chop action is employed but, at the moment of contact, when your bat is about to strike severely underneath the ball, you actually *ease-off*, before continuing the follow through in the normal way. The ball will return as if it has been chopped, but in fact will carry very little backspin, if any.

ATTACKING STROKES

The Topspin Drive is the basic attacking stroke, and it can be made from either forehand or backhand. Again the sideways stance is the ideal, weight starting on the back foot and being transferred to the front foot during the action.

Forehand

Start with the bat held at waist height and just behind the body and aim to make contact with the approaching ball when it arrives at a point roughly level with your body. On contact the arm and bat should start to move forward and upward, following through until the bat reaches a forward position at, or just below, head-height. The body turns from the waist as the stroke is made, so that on completion your shoulders will be almost square-on to the table.

Once again, allowance must be made for the speed, and type of spin employed by your opponent. This is done by adjusting your bat angle and your wrist movement to a degree which only experience will

Peter's Topspin Forehand—approach.   Peter's Topspin Forehand—contact.

44

enable you to determine. However, the bat tilt need not be so exaggerated as for a topspin service, since this time the ball will be travelling towards you.

Peter's Topspin Forehand—
follow-through.

Backhand

The movements for the ideal backhand topspin drive are very similar to the forehand, though with the feet reversed of course. Contact is normally made a little earlier and, since less turn of the trunk is involved, the wrist may be turned on contact to give an extra boost to the topspin imparted on the ball.

The vast majority of players favour forehand as opposed to backhand play and, it being virtually impossible to give equal attention to both at match-play speed, there is an understandable tendency for players to

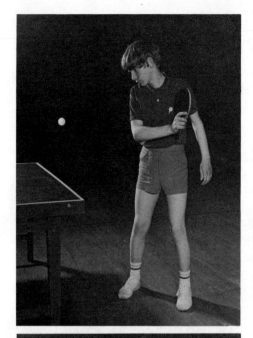

46

TOP LEFT:

Jill's Topspin Forehand follow-through when using ordinary pimpled rubber bat.

TOP RIGHT:

As above—Backhand.

Note in each case her bat finishes above her head level.

BOTTOM LEFT:

Peter's Block-Flick—Approach.

modify the sideways stance for backhand shots to one which is halfway between the ideal and 'square-on'. This is perfectly practical and sensible, so long as the player realises that, by taking the ball towards the front of his body instead of the side, he will not be able to get any real power into his backhand shot. Should he attempt to do so the ball would almost certainly miss the end of the table. Regard the modified backhand stance simply as a convenient device for staying in business, and assisting you to bring your stronger forehand topspin into play as rapidly and conveniently as possible.

Peter's Block-Flick—Follow-through, with his bat coming across.

Another type of backhand shot now in use at the top level is what might be described as the *Block-Flick*. The ball is taken very early, almost on the half-volley, there is an extra flick of the arm and the wrist is broken on contact so that the bat is brought across the top of the ball to impart some sidespin as well as topspin. Though it is more of a block than a flick, used with surprise and carefully placed, this shot can often catch an opponent completely off guard.

There are several modifications of this kind which may suit your game, but once more I would stress the advisability of learning the ideal method first, the main principles of which will remain important even when applied to a less exaggerated degree.

DUMMY TOPSPIN

Denis Neale, one of England's leading players, has a favourite shot which often bamboozles opponents during a counter-hitting rally. He shapes to play an orthodox backhand topspin shot, which he will follow through in the normal way, but at the moment his bat actually contacts the ball he deliberately eases off in his action. In effect he is producing a backspin return with a topspin action, and here's why:—

As we have seen, topspin makes the ball travel forward and spin in a forward direction, while backspin makes the ball move forward but spin backwards. The ball that Denis received will be charged with his opponent's topspin, so that it spins towards him. By easing off on contact with his own topspin action, the ball he returns will still be carrying a proportion of that spin originally imparted by his opponent. When Denis's opponent comes to deal with this ball it will be travelling towards him, but rotating backwards. If he fails to read this correctly as back-spin, he will almost certainly play his shot down instead of up, and so put the ball into the net.

HALF-VOLLEY

Besides being an emergency defensive stroke, used at the right moment, well placed, and given a little push with the sandwich bat, the half volley can be a valuable attacking ploy, sometimes a point-winner.

It is normally played on the backhand wing, and nearly always over the body, rather than from the full sideways stance. There is very little

49

Jill's half-volley made with sandwich bat.   Jill's half-volley made with ordinary pimpled bat.

approach movement of arm and bat, the bat being presented to the ball and held close to the table surface, contact being made with a block and slight forward push at the instant the ball bounces. There is very little follow through.

Once again the bat should be tilted to suit the spin and speed employed by your opponent. When meeting topspin the bat should be tilted forward, while for backspin it should be tilted backwards.

DROP SHOT

Imagine you have been making a series of hard top spin forehand drives, forcing your opponent further and further back from the table edge in his

Peter's Drop Shot—Contact.   Peter's Drop Shot—Follow-through.

defensive action. Then comes a backspin return which is a little shorter. Once more you shape to drive the ball deep into his court, but just before contact you arrest the forward motion of your bat, slide it quickly underneath the ball and lift it gently just over the net.

This is the drop shot, the most deadly yet most difficult of all·shots to produce. Basically, it is a short return placed only an inch or two the other side of the net which bounces as little as possible either forward or upward. Used delicately and accurately, in the circumstances described above, it should achieve complete surprise and spreadeagle your opponent. But it should be used sparingly, or it loses surprise value, and preferably be combined with the topspin attack when a fairly low return falls close to the net, as in the example given. Under other circumstances,

51

or if not properly disguised, it might simply provide your opponent with an easy 'kill'.

Most find the forehand drop shot easier to do than the backhand, and you'll find the full sideways stance is a help. In fact this is scarcely a shot at all, because you relax your grip just before contact and 'give' to the ball, absorbing most of the speed from your opponent's shot, so that the ball just creeps over the net. However, the most delicate 'touch' is required.

Even if you lack the 'feather touch' to use the drop shot as a point winner, its employment in a slightly modified form can be a useful tactical weapon to get your opponent off balance for a kill.

Any return arriving your side of the table at a height above net level is a candidate for the flat hit, an attacking shot played without imparting

THE KILL

The Flat Hit: note how Jill is bringing her bat down on the ball.

Jill's follow-through after the Kill.

spin, travelling straight to a point where your opponent cannot reach it.

This is the 'kill', and once applied no reply is expected. Learn to 'kill' with absolute certainty; if you can't you won't win many matches. And don't miss the slightest opportunity of using it.

The sideways stance should be used, and the bat brought flat against the ball when it is at the peak of its bounce, moving along the path you intend the ball to follow.

CHOP SMASH

If you find that your 'kills' are not all coming off as they should, and for occasional variety against a high, short return without much backspin, the Chop Smash is a useful weapon to have up your sleeve.

The Chop Smash. Jill's approach.

The Chop Smash. Jill's follow-through.

A normal backspin defensive swing is used, except that it should start much higher and the ball must be struck at the peak of its bounce. Bring the bat forcibly down and forward, and aim to place your shot just over the net and wide of your opponent. The spin tends to make the ball soar, so there is a danger of missing the end of the table if you aim too deep.

THE LOOP

The topspin loop is produced on similar lines to the normal topspin drive but from more of a crouching position, often some distance from the table edge. It also requires a much more accentuated action and follow-through, to give the ball unexpected 'kick' after bouncing. There are two basic types—High Loop and Low Loop.

When first introduced into international play by the Japanese in the 1950's, the Loop caused havoc among players unfamiliar with the intricacies of its spin. Today, however, it has become a basic stroke of the game, no longer necessarily an outright point-winner, but as a variation capable of forcing a loose return.

It is a spin which can still frighten a player meeting it for the first time, or one unfamiliar with the technique necessary to deal with it. First try to understand its nature—it is a tremendous amount of top-spin which has been imparted by striking the back of the ball very severely with an upward motion of the bat.

High Loop

This was the first type to be introduced into the game, and it is widely used against slow backspin returns. To produce it, the bat travels

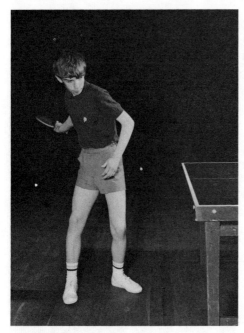
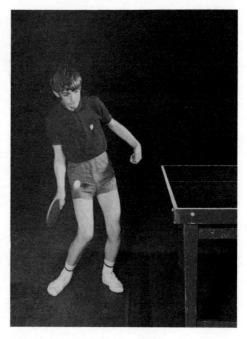

High Loop. Peter's approach.

High Loop. Just before contact.

vertically upwards, finishing way above the head. At precisely the right moment during its passage the bat must brush the top of the ball very severely. Timing must be spot on, since it is easy to miss the ball altogether (this happens quite frequently, even in top international play). However, a correctly executed High Loop will cause the ball to lift some three or four feet over the net and, after bouncing, kick off the table.

Low Loop

After a while, leading players found they could add the loop to their fast attacking shots; the Low Loop is the result. The main difference

55

in production is that the path of the bat should be *forward* and upward, in fact more forward than upward. The margin for error in timing is improved by the fact that a larger area of the ball (both the top and the back) will this time be brushed on contact.

High Loop. Follow-through.

Whereas the High Loop relies only on spin for effect, the Low Loop has the added advantages of versatility and speed.

Returning the Loop

One effective way of returning the Loop is to take the ball very late after a good deal of the spin has died away. This means chop defence at

Chopping the Loop from long range, i.e. taking the ball very late. Jill's approach (Forehand).

As above—follow-through.

As previous page—the approach for the Backhand Chop.

Follow-through to Backhand Chop as shown above.

58

long range, and even at long range from the table edge it is necessary to stroke the ball downward as if seeking to chop the ball into the net.

An alternative is to use the *half-volley smother* shot. Take the ball very early, as you would a normal half-volley, but on contact close the bat over the top of the ball and *force* the ball downwards. Close-to-the-table players will favour this method.

There is a third method for dealing with the Low Loop which is 'Looping the Loop', but this is a very advanced technique which I would advise you to forget for the time being.

Dummy Loop

Peter's half-volley smother shot—forehand.

A cunning tactic is to pretend to make a high loop stroke but at the moment of contact, instead of striking the ball severely, ease right off in the action. The follow-through, however, should be continued as for the normal High Loop.

The ball will return at the height expected for a High Loop, but carrying much less topspin than usual. If your opponent should buy this dummy, treating it as if it were a High Loop, his return is pretty certain to shoot into the bottom of the net.

Recognised in time, the dummy should be treated as an ordinary topspin return. If confidently read, it can be promptly killed.

Peter's half-volley smother shot—backhand.

TACTICS

After watching England's Denis Neale in action during an international match, a youngster asked me: 'Why should I bother to learn a large number of different strokes when one of England's best players uses only two?'.

Fair enough. It is true that Denis Neale might play a whole series of important matches using only two main strokes, his backhand merely to set up opportunities to use his very powerful forehand drive. But the day comes when Denis's normal tactics just won't work, and then he is obliged to play an entirely different sort of game. A good example was Denis's vital match for England against Austria in a 1968 European League match. Denis's opponent, though regarded as a player of lesser ability, hit an inspired patch. He looked capable of countering successfully any attacking move that the Englishman was able to make.

Philosophically, Denis accepted the fact that his best shot wasn't coming off and decided immediately to change his tactics. In doing this he was applying a golden rule of matchplay—'Know your limitations'—and this also means 'at any particular time'. Casting aside his familiar two-stroke attacking patterns, he fell back and concentrated entirely on backspin defence, something few of us had seen him employ before, and which he may not need to use again for years to come. However the skill was there, waiting to be called upon when needed, and on this occasion it swung the match and brought Denis a memorable victory.

There you have one good reason for practising every stroke in the book until it becomes instinctive, and available for use when required.

You can practice all your strokes, and stroke-combinations in a scientific manner with the aid of a friend.

In modern match playing of a high standard there is a golden rule which needs special emphasis. Whatever stroke you are playing, aim to return the ball either short or deep and *never* to the middle of the table. The reason is that most players are now so advanced that they can 'kill' any ball of mid-table length.

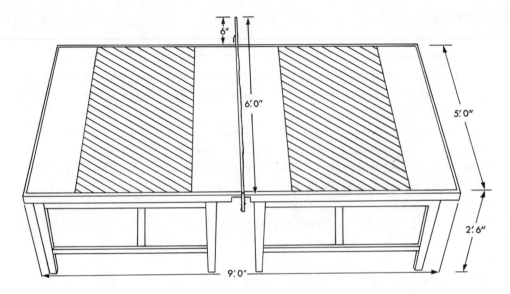

Never return a ball to the middle of the table (which is the shaded area shown in this diagram).

In time you will develop your own individual style of play, but whether you will be able to impose it on your particular opponent or not cannot be determined until play starts. Be ready to switch tactics, or develop new tactics on the spot.

In the 1960's, attacking players were very much in the ascendant, but in future defenders may well start to come back into their own. These things tend to go in cycles, and need not bother you. At all times the secret is to work for openings to use your own best shots, whatever they may be.

As you have seen, backspin is the normal counter to topspin, and vice versa, but it is perfectly possible to employ topspin against topspin (counter-hitting) by angling the bat well forward and striking the ball

This, and the next picture show the vulnerability of an all-forehand style. Peter is shown making a forehand attacking shot from the extreme backhand wing . . .

. . . next he is forced to move across to the extreme forehand wing to play an angled return. He does this quite successfully, but will now be vulnerable to a sudden return down his backhand wing.

near its top and as it is rising. One can also return backspin with back-spin (chopping the chop) by bringing the bat horizontally forward under the ball and tilting the forward edge of your bat upward on contact.

Forehand shots need not all be made from the forehand wing, nor backhand from the backhand, but can be made from any part of the court.

Then again, the drop shot and a whole range of 'dummy' shots can be used to fool your opponent.

It is by variation and surprise that you can upset the rhythm of the exchanges and so cause an opponent to misread your shots and mis-time his own.

A good tip is to play to an opponent's strength, but to score your winners through his weakness. Take a penhold opponent, for example. The penholder grips the handle of his bat between his first finger and thumb and makes all shots from the same side of his bat. His strength is forehand hitting from all parts of the court, his weakness a backhand which is virtually non-existent, or at best decidedly cramped. Only a handful of Asiatic penhold stars are able to produce a stylish backhand.

Most probably he will take up position to receive your service on his extreme backhand wing, intent on returning the ball with a forehand hit no matter where it is placed, nor what spin it carries. Try sending the first ball wide down his forehand, and the next wide down his backhand side.

Another good gambit is the very short chop just over the net. The penholder always aims to start his swing below the table edge, and is less comfortable when dealing with the sudden, short return.

However, many penholders have abnormally fast footwork so you may need to ring the changes persistently over a period before getting the results you want.

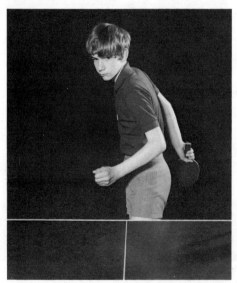 

To surprise his opponent, Peter adds Sidespin to his normal Topspin attack. The approach for a shot which, from his opponent's viewpoint, is going to break from left to right.

Peter's follow-through.

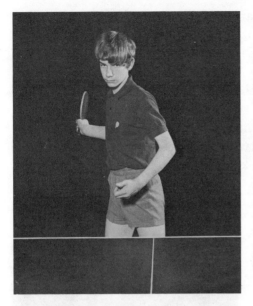

TOP LEFT:

An approach as in first picture opposite, but this time aiming to produce a right-to-left break from the opponent's viewpoint.

TOP RIGHT:

Peter's follow-through.

BOTTOM LEFT:

Left-handed Trevor Taylor, Peter's elder brother, playing his favourite backhand shot. He uses very little backswing in his approach, taking the ball early to try and spread his opponent.

65

As I have written previously, we are more concerned today with what gets good results than what just looks good. If you have a shot of your own which looks ugly but wins points consistently, then go ahead and use it at every possible opportunity. Remember, though, the day will come when your opponents will tumble you, and where will you be then?

It seems likely that the speed of our game has not reached its peak, so future improvement must come through speed of thought and variety of stroke play. The more complete your knowledge of how to produce, and how to counter the various strokes, the more versatile and effective your match tactics can be.

Note Trevor's generous follow-through, which is to compensate for his short initial backswing.

A good illustration of how cramped is the backhand of most Asiatic penhold players.

DOUBLES

Play to your opponents' weaknesses and your partner's strength—that's the golden rule in table tennis doubles which is an increasingly

Doubles. Jill and Peter, both right-handed, have decided to take their own courts, so while Jill serves Peter stands back to his partner's right side.

important championship event demanding exceptionally good teamwork and close understanding.

The main reason is the ball must be struck by each of the four players in turn. After you have struck the ball it is your partner who must receive the return.

To be able to make your shot and then leave the table clear for your partner, quick footwork to a previously agreed pattern is essential. One

Following, Jill after serving moves back and to her partner's left side,
Peter stepping in to play the next shot—a backhand.

method frequently used is to continue running through after completing each stroke. When one partner favours forehand and the other backhand, or in a right- and left-handed partnership, partners can conveniently occupy one half of the table each, without having to run round each other.

The thing to avoid is attempting to return to the position from which you started your stroke. If you do this your body will obscure your

Doubles. Left- (Trevor) and right-hander (Peter) in partnership. This is similar to the previous page. Peter leaves the court clear for Trevor to play a forehand, then . . .

partner's view of the ball. Another tip is to use the sideways-on stance whenever possible; it takes up less room and facilitates a quick get-away.

Suppose you are a defensive player partnering an attacker; your aim must be to induce your opponent to return the sort of loose ball that your partner can kill.

. . . Trevor steps back and to one side leaving ample room for brother Peter
to step forward and play the next shot.

The rule about 'order of play' is a bit hard to follow, but needs your
attention. Imagine that A and B are playing a 3-game match against
C and D, and have won the right to serve first. They decide between
them (as the serving pair are entitled to do in every game) that A should
open the serving, whereupon their opponents nominate C to receive.
For the rest of that game the playing order is then established. A serves

Doubles—the Circling method. Peter plays a forehand, meantime Jill moves round behind him.

to C, then C to A, B to D, and D to B. After this A serves to C again, and so on.

In the next game the order of receiving must be opposite to that of the preceding game, so that if C and D nominate C to open the serving the, first receiver must be B. B then automatically becomes first server of the A and B partnership for the rest of that game.

In the third and final game, when either pair reaches the score 10 the

Circling (2) Jill moves in to play a backhand shot while Peter circles behind her.

receiving pair must alter its order of serving.

What happens at the score of 20-20? The sequence of serving and receiving remains uninterrupted, but each player is allowed only one service in turn until the end of the game.

If you win the toss, should you choose 'end' or 'service'? There is not necessarily any advantage to be gained from either. However, if the opposing pair are well known to you, you may decide to let them serve

Circling (3) Peter completes the circle by moving in to play another shot while Jill is about to circle again behind her partner.

first so you can have the order in your favour in the first game, and for the first ten points of a third and deciding game; so having the opportunity of making a flying start.

On the other hand, you might decide that it would be better for you to serve first, before your opponents have settled down, and take a chance that they will choose the order you want. Should your tactics misfire you can still count on having the order you prefer for the last ten points of a third and deciding game.

Doubles—the In and Out method. Peter is about to serve, while Jill stands
back from the backhand court.

There are three alternative standard positions for serving, or receiving
service. In choosing which to adopt you will be guided by your known
strengths and weaknesses as a pair.

A strong forehand player normally takes up a central position to serve
or receive, while his partner who is stronger on the backhand wing
waits behind him and to his right.

If it is the strong backhand player who is serving or receiving, he will

Peter, having served, steps back out of the way, while Jill moves in to make the next shot.

favour standing outside the right-hand corner to play his backhand while his partner waits on his left.

When players have decided to take their own courts, the server or receiver will be nearer the table than his partner, so after making his shot he must move either further to the right, or back and to the right. This last method demands the closest understanding between partners, but gives the server or receiver more freedom of choice in his stroke.

75

Once the rally starts, positioning depends on pre-determined tactics and the course of the game.

Obviously, the best doubles players are those who require very little space or movement to play their shots successfully.

TRAINING, FITNESS AND PRACTICE

Lapping, sprinting, skipping, deep breathing—these were my main activities when training for World Championship play. Often I trained with the professional footballers.

Though these fundamental exercises are still valuable and important, training today is far more scientific and specialised for table tennis, as it is for other sports where the speed and physical effort expended in play is ever increasing.

Special Circuit Training exercises have been devised which all table tennis players are recommended to carry out regularly at home, or in organised squads. Progress can be checked by performing these exercises against the clock. These are enjoyable, and do not involve heavy, or long periods of work. Many can be used as a means of 'warming up' before an important match.

The three main things to work on are Strength, Mobility and Stamina, and I am indebted to Les Gresswell, the coach and P.E. Expert who helps to supervise the training of the England squad, for the notes which follow:—

Ages 10-14

A child is growing rapidly at this stage, so a careful and individual programme is necessary. The normal school P.E. Syllabus should

76

provide sound basic fitness, but in addition there are many additional exercises which can be carried out to promote *quickness*.

These can take the form of quick, explosive running and general body movements used in team games.

The main aim of training at the 10-14 stage is to make the player aware of what the various parts of his body are doing during a game.

Ages 14-18

During the 14-18 period the pattern can be set for the hard, calculated training methods which follow. Strengthening, mobilising and speeding up of movements can all be approached in a serious manner.

For this type of training to be really beneficial it must be carried out regularly, at least twice a week. Also, a satisfactory balanced training period should last for one hour.

It is best to start with light work, gradually building up to a higher level by increasing the repetitions carried out.

There is no reason why training should not be done at home, with improvised equipment should better facilities not be available.

Strength

Make yourself strong all over by using light weights to carry out light exercises. The more repetitions you do, the stronger you will get.

Mobility

Mobility is, of course, essential for co-ordinated movement. Flexibility can be obtained and maintained by exercising for just five minutes every day.

Stamina

Stamina centres around running to get the heart beating more slowly. This promotes the endurance necessary to last out in lengthy tournaments.

To develop all three of these essential requirements for competitive table tennis, here are three exercises which will be found of great benefit if performed daily:—

1. *Wrist Curl*
A light weight is tied to one end of a length of rope, at the other end of which is tied a rod which you hold in both hands. Light weights are important: 5 lbs. for girls, 8 lbs. for boys.

The object is to lift the weight gradually upwards by winding the rope around the rod.

You will find that this exercise strengthens the wrists and forearms to add power and control to your table tennis strokes.

2. *Trunk Raising*
Lying face downwards, stomach supported by a bench and feet tucked under an adjacent wall bar, clasp a light weight at the back of your neck.

The object is to raise the chest up and down, holding the body still at the top of each movement for a few seconds.

This strengthens and mobilises the back, and chest muscles, and also helps the shoulder joint to remain flexible. Table tennis players use trunk and shoulder muscles in the arm swing.

3. *Bench Push*
Lie on your back underneath a bench, the top of which is securely fastened to a wall bar. Start with your feet under the bottom end of the bench.

The object is to raise the bottom end of the bench upwards by straightening the legs, then to repeat the movement quickly.

This strengthens the leg muscles and keeps the knee joints supple. If the toes are put against the bench, this helps to strengthen the ankles. Knees, legs and ankles are constantly in use in table tennis.

Here are members of the England international squad pictured during training. Among the exercises being performed are the Wrist Curl, Trunk Raising, and the Bench Push (as described in the text).

Here are some daily routine tasks and suggested pre-match warming-up exercises recommended by the E.T.T.A.:—

Daily Routine and Suggested Pre-match Exercises

These exercises should be performed daily and occupy a time of between 10-15 minutes. The whole purpose of these exercises will be completely negative unless conducted properly and regularly, with the 'maximum' effort.

Introduction

The tasks set are designed for mobility and flexibility of the parts of the body considered dominant in table tennis.

Technique

1 Aim—to mobilise the trunk and hips.
2 Lying on the back with arms at side.
3 Legs go over back of the head so that the feet are touching the floor.
4 Try to walk 'around' your body, working from side to side.

1 Aim—mobilising trunk.
2 Apparatus—a ball or some form of light weight.
3 Sitting position, legs on the floor.
4 Object held in both hands.
5 Alternate from side to side, placing the ball directly behind back.

1 Aim—making hips and leg ligaments supple.
2 Standing position, front leg forward (bent), back leg straight—as far as possible.
3 Push weight on front leg, still keeping legs stretched and back leg straight.
4 Alternate legs.

1 Aim—flexing leg and stomach muscles.
2 Sitting position, legs as wide apart as possible.
3 Touch toes, alternate with both hands.
4 Legs on floor, bend trunk forward.

1 Aim—improve muscles for a free and easy 'arm-swing'.
2 Standing position, preferably with back to a firm support but one which will allow a free arm-swing (e.g. edge of a door).
3 Arms by side, swing freely upwards and when at the top of the swing (e.g. when there is resistance) push back (3 times).

4 Repeat, building up rhythm.

1 Aim—loosening arm socket and giving slight assistance to forearm.
2 Standing position, arms bent in, fingers on chest, forearms are held level.
3 Arms straighten and are held at shoulder level, pushed back three times.
4 Repeat, with rhythm.

Pre-match Method

Introduction

The whole purpose of these simple tasks is merely to prepare the necessary physical parts to be ready for the 'explosive' action during the game. They should be performed very lightly and serve not only as a 'warming up' system but also a relaxing factor. If possible, leave a few minutes to adjust before the game.

Technique
1 Standing position, feet apart, hands on hips.
2 Bending trunk, rotate sideways and then forwards so that the trunk makes a complete circle.
3 Keep legs apart and hands on hips.

1 Standing position.
2 Squatting in crouch position and straightening up.
3 Keep body upright.

1 Standing upright, legs apart.
2 Moving trunk directly to the side without bending hips or body forward.

3 Reach down with arm on the bending side, while bringing the other arm up under the arm pit.
4 Repeat alternate sides.

1 Standing upright jogging on the toes.
2 Arms out-stretched, full swing forwards and backwards (not alternate).
3 Keep body upright.

1 Hold hands loosely together in front of body.
2 Forearms and elbows together.
3 Move vigorously from side to side, flexing the wrists over at each side movement.
4 Keep feet moving.

Conclusion

The flexing and curling of the fingers is very important at all times, especially before a game. Finally, it must be remembered that these exercises should be performed in a relaxed manner and without stress.

Pressure Training

Routine training on the lines as previously indicated by Les Gresswell is being carried out by table tennis players all over the world, but in addition special methods of Pressure Training have been evolved which are suitable for the advanced player who wishes to compete successfully at the very highest level.

Once again, the exercises are enjoyable but need to be carried out with serious determination if mental and physical capacity is to be improved. These are for two or more players.

The programme starts with simple limbering up to loosen neck, wrists, arms, shoulders, trunk, knees and ankles. Next come the basic movements used in play—turning to backhand and forehand from the basic 'ready position'; moving to the left and right when facing the table; moving in, and out, on the forehand and backhand lines. Then essential movements are combined, such as the left-right movement with the in-out. All this is done under the supervision of a qualified coach.

'On the Table' practice starts with an all-round warm-up session for the entire squad using 3 or more balls, then concentrates on individual stroke production. The coach may make a series of varied services to all points of the table, inviting each player to practice various returns such as the half-volley block, slow push, and so on. He may make a series of steady push returns, requiring the players to direct his shots to a certain target area.

Pressure is gradually increased, the player being required to alternate between forehand and backhand while the coach alternates between slow, and half-volley 'push' returns.

Next come stroke combinations on one line of play, such as forehand drive alternated with forehand push while the coach makes chop and push returns on the same line; then combinations which involve turning, such as the short backhand push alternated with long forehand chop, all balls returning to a specified target area, while the coach alternates a drop shot to one target with a topspin drive to another. All the time pressure is gradually being increased.

Finally there are really advanced practices involving sidespin, variations, angled push play and counter-hitting, looped topspin, and topspin as defence.

There is no reason why you should not devise your own games for fun, and to improve your strokes, speed and mobility, at the same time. For example, you and your opponent could play a game 21-up under the special rule that every shot must be played backhand—this can be exhausting! Then there is the exciting party game of rounders, suitable for when about twenty players are involved and only two bats, one ball, and one table are available. Players circle the table in single file, each picking up the bat as his turn comes to play the ball, then replacing it on the table and moving on quickly to make room for the next man. One false stroke and you are eliminated.

In the closing stages, when only a few players remain, they really have to race round the table to grab the bat in time to play their shots.

England players at pressure training. Jill's task here is to return a service, then at once run back, touch the wall behind her with her bat, and return to the table in time to cope with the next service. The server, equipped with a stock of balls, times his services to ensure maximum effort from Jill.

Ultimately, when only two players remain, one point is played to determine the winner.

The England team use a slight variation of this party game. We employ three or four tables, each being manned at one end only. Players are required to run from table to table, and make the appropriate returns.

The way we play, this game is strictly for the very fit!

ENGLISH TABLE TENNIS ASSOCIATION
LAWS OF TABLE TENNIS (abbreviated version)

1 The Table

The table shall be in surface rectangular, 9ft in length and 5ft in width; it shall be supported so that its upper surface, termed the 'playing surface', shall lie in a horizontal plane 2ft 6in. above the floor. It shall be made of any material and shall yield a uniform bounce of not less then $8\frac{3}{4}$in. and not more than $9\frac{3}{4}$in. when a standard ball is dropped from a height of 12in. above its surface. The playing surface shall be dark coloured, preferably dark green, and matt, with a white line $\frac{3}{4}$in. broad along each edge. The lines at the 5ft edges, or ends, shall be termed 'end lines', and the lines at the 9ft edges, or side, shall be termed 'side lines'.

For doubles, the playing surface shall be divided into two halves by a white line $\frac{1}{8}$in. broad, running parallel to the side lines, termed the 'centre line'. The centre line may, for convenience, be permanently marked in full length on the table and this in no way invalidates the table for singles play.

2 The Net and its Supports

The playing surface shall be divided into two courts of equal size by a net running parallel to the end lines. The net, with its suspension, shall be 6ft in length; along its whole length its upper part shall be 6in. above the playing surface and its lower part shall be close to the playing surface. It shall be suspended by a cord attached at each end to an upright post 6in. high; the outside limits of each post shall be 6in. outside the side line.

3 The Ball

The ball should be spherical, with a diameter of not less than 1.46in. and not more than 1.50in. It shall be made of celluloid or a similar plastic, white and matt; it shall be not less than 37 grains and not more than 39 grains in weight.

4 The Racket

The racket may be of any size, shape or weight. Its surface shall be dark coloured and matt. The blade shall be of wood, continuous, of even thickness, flat and rigid. If the blade is covered on either side, this covering may be either plain, ordinary pimpled rubber, with pimples outward, of a total thickness of not more than 2mm., or 'sandwich', consisting of a layer of cellular rubber surfaced by plain, ordinary pimpled rubber, turned inwards or outwards, of a total thickness of not more than 4mm. When rubber is used on both sides of a racket, the colours on the two sides shall be similar; when wood is used for either side it should be dark, either naturally or by being stained, but not painted, in such a way as not to change the friction character of the surface.

The part of the blade nearest the handle and gripped by the fingers may be covered with any material for convenience of grip, and is to be regarded as part of the handle. Similarly, if the reverse side of the racket is never used for striking the ball it may be covered with any material as the limitation of covering materials applies only to the striking surface; a stroke with a side covered with any material other than those specified above would, however, be illegal and result in a lost point.

5 Order of Play: Definitions

The period during which the ball is in play shall be termed a 'rally'. A rally the result of which is not scored shall be termed a 'let', and a rally the result of which is scored shall be termed a 'point'.

The player who first strikes the ball during a rally shall be termed the 'server', and the player who next strikes the ball shall be termed the 'receiver'. In singles, the server shall first make a good service, the receiver shall then make a good return and thereafter server and receiver shall each alternately make a good return.

In doubles, the server shall first make a good service, the receiver shall then make a good return, the partner of the server shall then make a good return, the partner of the receiver shall then make a good return and there after each player alternately in that sequence shall make a good return.

6 A Good Service

The ball shall be placed on the palm of the free hand, which must be stationary. Service shall commence by the server projecting the ball by hand only, without imparting spin, near vertically upwards, so that the ball is visible at all times to the umpire and so that it visibly leaves the palm. As the ball is descending from the height of its trajectory it shall be struck so that it touch first the server's court and then, passing directly over or around the net, touch the receiver's court.

In doubles, the ball shall touch first the server's right half-court or the centre line on his side of the net and then, passing directly over or around the net, touch the receiver's right half-court or the centre line on his side of the net. The free hand, while in contact with the ball in service shall be above the level of the playing surface and shall be open, with the fingers together and thumb free, the ball resting on the palm without being cupped or pinched in any way by the fingers. Strict observance of the prescribed method of service may be waived where the umpire is notified before play begins, that compliance by the player in question is prevented by physical disability.

At the moment of the impact of the racket on the ball in service, the ball shall be behind the end line or an imaginary extension thereof.

NOTES: 1. 'Struck' means 'hit with the racket or with the racket hand below the wrist'. The 'racket hand' is the hand carrying the racket, and the 'free hand' is the hand not carrying the racket. Therefore, a stroke made with the hand alone, after dropping the racket, is 'not good', for it is no longer the 'racket hand'; a stroke made by the racket alone, after it has slipped or been thrown from the hand is likewise 'not good', for the ball is not 'struck'.

2. The phrase 'playing surface', is to be interpreted as including the top edges of the table-top, and a ball in play which strikes these latter is therefore still in play; if however, it strikes the side of the table-top below the edge it becomes out of play and counts against the last striker.

3. 'Around the net' shall be considered as being under or around the projection of the net and supports outside the side line. The net end should be close enough to the post to prevent the ball from passing between the net and post and to pass so would not be regarded as 'around the net'.

4. If a player, in attempting to serve, miss the ball altogether he loses the point, because the ball was in play from the moment it left his hand and a good service has not been made of the ball in play.

7 A Good Return

The ball having been served or returned in play shall be struck so that it pass directly over or around the net and touch directly the opponent's court, provided that if the ball, having been served or returned in play, return with its own impetus over or around the net it may be struck while still in play so that it touch directly the opponent's court. If the ball, in passing over or around the net, touch it or its supports it shall be considered to have passed directly.

8 In Play

The ball is in play from the moment at which it is projected from the hand in service until:—

(a) it has touched one court twice consecutively.

(b) it has, except in service, touched each court alternately without having been struck with the racket intermediately.

(c) it has been struck by a player more than once consecutively.

(d) it has touched a player or anything he wears or carries.

(e) it has come into contact with the racket or the racket hand below the wrist not yet having touched the playing surface on one side of the net since last being struck on the other side, when it shall be said to have been 'volleyed'.

(f) it has touched any object other than the net, supports, or those referred to above.

(g) it has, in a doubles service, touched the left half-court of the server or of the receiver.

(h) it has, in doubles, been struck by a player out of proper sequence except as provided in Law 15.

9 A Let

The rally is a let:—

(a) if the ball served, in passing over the net, touch it or its supports, provided the service be otherwise good or be volleyed by the receiver.

(b) if a service be delivered when the receiver or his partner is not ready, provided always that a player may not be deemed to be unready if he or his partner attempt to strike at the ball.

(c) if, owing to an accident not within his control, a player fail to make a good service or a good return, or otherwise terminate the rally.

(d) if it be interrupted for correction of a mistake in playing order or ends.

(e) if it be interrupted for application of the Expedite System.

NOTES: 1. If the ball become fractured in play, affecting a player's return, the rally is a let. It is the umpire's duty to stop play, recording a let, imperfect; he must also decide whether the ball is fractured in going out of play and in no way handicaps the player's return, when the point should be scored. In all cases of doubt he should declare a let.

2. A moving spectator, a neighbouring object or player other than a partner in movement or a sudden noise should be regarded as an accident not within control of the player, interference from which implies a let. A stationary spectator, the umpire, the light, a nearby table, a continuous sound of even volume, or any such relatively constant or motionless hazard should not be so regarded and complaint against interference from it during the play should be regarded as void.

3. If a game be unfinished fifteen minutes after it has begun, the rest of the game and the remaining games of the match shall proceed under the Expedite System. At the end of fifteen minutes the umpire shall interrupt play by calling 'let'. If the interruption occurs during a rally the game shall be re-started by service from the player who served in the rally that was interrupted; if the interruption occurs between rallies the game shall be re-started by service from the player who received in the preceding rally. The return strokes of the receiving player or pair shall be counted out loud, from one to thirteen by an official other than the umpire.

10 A Point

Except as provided in Law 9, a player shall lose a point:—

(a) if he fail to make a good service.

(b) if, a good service or a good return having been made by his opponent, he fail to make a good return.

(c) if he, or his racket, or anything that he wears or carries, touch the net or its supports while the ball is in play.

(d) if he, or his racket, or anything that he wears or carries, move the playing surface while the ball is in play.

(e) if his free hand touch the playing surface while the ball is in play.

(f) if, before the ball in play shall have passed over the end lines or side lines not yet having touched the playing surface on his side of the net since being struck by his opponent, it come in contact with him or with anything he wears or carries.

(g) if he volley the ball.

(h) if, in doubles, he strike the ball out of proper sequence, except as provided in Law 15.

(i) if, under the Expedite System, his service and the twelve following strokes of the serving player or pair be returned by good returns of the receiving player or pair.

11 A Game

A game shall be won by the player or pair first scoring 21 points, unless both players or pairs shall have scored 20 points, when the winner of the game shall be the player or pair first scoring 2 points more than the opposing player or pair.

12 A Match

A match shall consist of one game, the best of three or the best of five games, play shall be continuous throughout, except that either player or pair is entitled to claim a repose period of not more than five minutes duration between the third and fourth games of a five game match.

13 The Choice of Ends and Service

The choice of ends and the right to serve or receive first in a match shall be decided by toss, provided that, if the winner of the toss choose the right to serve or receive first the loser shall have the choice of ends and vice versa, and provided that the winner of the toss may, if he prefer it, require the loser to make first choice.

In doubles, the pair who have the right to serve the first five services in any game shall decide which partner shall do so. In the first game of a match the opposing pair shall then decide similarly which shall be the first receiver. In subsequent games the serving pair shall choose their first server and the first receiver will then be established automatically to correspond with the first server as provided in Law 14.

14 The Change of Ends and Service

The player or pair who started at one end in a game shall start at the other in the immediately subsequent game and so on, until the end of the match. In the last possible game of the match the players or pairs shall change ends when first either player or pair reaches the score 10.

In singles, after five points the receiver shall become the server and the server the receiver, and so on until the end of the game, except as provided below. In doubles, the first five services shall be delivered by the selected partner of the pair who have the right to do so and shall be received by the appropriate partner of the opposing pair. The second five services shall be delivered by the receiver of the first five services and received by the partner of the first server. The third five services shall be delivered by the partner of the first server and received by the partner of the first receiver. The fourth five services shall be delivered by the partner of the first receiver and received by the first server. The fifth five services shall be delivered as the first five and so on, in sequence, until the end of the game except as provided below.

From the score 20-all, or if the game is being played under the

Expedite System, the sequence of serving and receiving shall be the same but each player shall deliver only one service in turn until the end of the game.

The player or pair who served first in a game shall receive first in the immediate subsequent game.

In the last possible game of the doubles match the receiving pair shall alter its order of receiving when first either pair reaches the score 10.

In each game of a doubles match the initial order of receiving shall be opposite to that in the preceding game.

15 Out of Order of Ends, Serving or Receiving

If the players have not changed ends when ends should have been changed, they shall change ends as soon as the mistake is discovered, unless a game has been completed since the error, when the error shall be ignored. In any circumstances, all points scored before the discovery shall be reckoned.

If by mistake a player serve or receive out of his turn, play shall be interrupted as soon as the mistake is discovered and shall continue with that player serving or receiving who, according to the sequence established at the beginning of the match or at the score 10 if that sequence has been changed as provided in Law 14, should be server or receiver respectively at the score that has been reached. In any circumstances, all points scored before the discovery shall be reckoned.

PROFICIENCY AWARDS

English players have the opportunity of testing their control of length and direction, and their general ability, by entering for the National Bronze Award. This can be taken at any convenient time under the supervision of an approved teacher or coach, and full details are available from: The English Table Tennis Association, 26-29 Park Crescent, London, W1. A modest entry fee is involved.

Having achieved the Bronze Certificate a player may take the Silver, then the Gold test which is assessed only at formal sessions organised by the E.T.T.A.

This Scheme is worthy of the special attention of international administrators, and all players, since it encourages a sound system of learning the game individually, or in a group.

For each test, a controller and scorer are appointed. The controller is a player able to place slow and steady balls to required targets, with required spin. The scorer keeps count of 'successes and errors'. An assessor will rule on quality of performance appropriate to each Test level. If only one item of a Test has been failed, a second attempt may be made on the same day. If two items are failed, or one failed twice, application must be made for a re-test.

Appropriate Target areas are shown *in the diagram*, A, B, C, D are Centre Points of the four 'courts'.

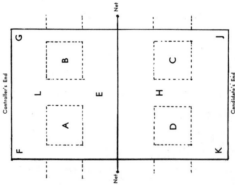

Area A is the Controller's Right-hand Centre Area (18 ins square)
Area B is the Controller's Left-hand Centre Area (18 ins square)
Area C is the Candidate's Right-hand Centre Area (18 ins square)
Area D is the Candidate's Left-hand Centre Area (18 ins square)

These may be marked by coins, or removable plastic tape. A good way to practice the tests is with two sheets of foolscap paper to form a useful approximation of the Centre Area.

To achieve the initial Bronze Award, a candidate must pass the following Test:

94

(a) *Short-Touch Services.* (i) Serve 5 Short Forehand Services, i.e. to land short of a line marked 18 inches from the net. (ii) As (i), but service with Backhand

Total 3 (for 10 successes)

(b) *Long Topspin Services.* (i) Serve 5 Long Forehand Topspin Services, i.e. to land within 18 inches of the distant baseline. (ii) As (i) but service with Backhand

Total 3 (for 10 successes)

(c) *All-Forehand Push-Control.* (From 2 points, returned to 1 target). Using sound footwork for training, return 40 Slow Push Shots, (which have been placed, slowly, by Controller, alternately to Area 'C' and Area 'D'). Candidate to use *only forehand push-strokes*, all played back to Controller's Area 'A'. (See diagram for Areas; Left-handed Candidates return all balls to Area 'B')

5

(d) *All-Backhand Push-Control.* (From 2 points, returned to 1 target). As (c) but Candidate to use *only backhand push-strokes*, and to return all balls to Controller's Area 'B'. (Left-handed Candidates return all balls to Area 'A')

5

(e) *Forehand and Backhand Push-Control (alternated).* Return 40 Slow pushes by playing *backhand push and forehand push strokes, strictly alternately* and with due attention to correct execution, all balls to be kept within a channel 18 inches wide.

5

NOTE: For 'Penholder' Styles, for 'Backhand' read: 'To Left of the Body'.

A small, but reasonable margin for error is allowed.

More advanced strokes, and stroke combinations are involved in the Silver Test, and in addition ten questions are asked on the Laws, but there is nothing to cause undue worry to any player who has reached a sound, all-round standard.

Preliminary: Candidate must have passed the 'Bronze' Award

(a) *Return of Service by Half-Volley.* (i) Using *backhand half-volley block-shot*, return safely 10 Services, varied as to Topspin and Chop. (ii) As (i) but using *forehand half-volley block-shot. Note:* Candidate may be asked to receive either of these tests in either Backhand or Forehand Court. This will enable two tests to be carried out simultaneously on one Table

Total 5 (for 20 successes)

(b) *Combining Drive-and-Push, Forehand.* Return 40 balls, which have been alternately chopped and pushed, by using (respectively) *topspin drives and push-shots*, played alternately, Forehand. *Note:* Candidate may be asked to control the play on 1 diagonal line, e.g. Areas 'C' to 'A', *or* 'D' to 'B'

5

(c) *Combining Drive-and-Push . . . Backhand.* As (b) but using *backhand* throughout

5

(d) *Combining (Chopped) Defensive Returns with Push, Forehand.* Return 40 balls, which have been alternately *driven* and *pushed*, on same line, by using, respectively *backspin defensive returns*, and *pushes*, played alternately, on same line, all *forehand*

5

(e) *Combining (Chopped) Defensive Returns with Push . . . Backhand.* As (d) but using *backhand* throughout

5

(f) *Laws of Table Tennis.* Answer 10 questions on the Laws of Table Tennis. *Note:* Assessors should allow 3 points for completely satisfactory answer; 2 points for correct 'sense'; 1 point for part answer. The Pass score is 22 out of 30

(g) *Maintaining Attack against Topspin.* (i) Maintain 10 triple sequences thus: *2 forehand drives* plus 1 *backhand block*. All balls returned on same line without pressure. (ii) As (i) but sequences of 2 *backhand drives* plus 1 *forehand block*

3

3

NOTE: For 'Penholder' Styles, for 'Backhand' read: 'To left of the body'

The Gold Test is for the advanced student who can perform accurately all the strokes, including the Drop Shot and Loop, sometimes in combination, and most times under pressure.

Preliminary: Candidate must have passed the 'Silver' Award
Candidate must pass 6 out of 8 Tests attempted

PERMITTED ERRORS

(a) *Topspin Driving under Pressure, Forehand.* Play 50 *forehand topspin drives*, to one point, against Half-Volley returns which have been placed *alternately* to each 'C' and 'D' Area (see Diagram). Good Forehand position and footwork required throughout — 4

(b) *Topspin Driving under Pressure . . . Backhand.* As (a) but using *backhand topspin drives* — 4

(c) *Counter-Driving, Close and Distant, Forehand.* Return 20 Counter-Drives by means of *forehand counter-drives*, in sequences of 2 thus: 2 'Close' 2 'Distant' 2 'Close' etc. all returns kept on the same line. — 2

(d) *Counter-Driving, Close and Distant . . . Backhand.* As (c), but using *backhand counter-drive* — 2

(e) *Combining Forehand and Backhand Topspin Drives.* Against slow chopped returns, which have been placed alternately just inside Forehand and Backhand corners, by playing 20 *forehand and backhand topspin drives*, alternately, directed just inside diagonally opposite corners — 2

(f) *Combining Forehand and Backhand Defensive Backspin Returns.* Return 20 Drives, received alternately on Forehand and Backhand corner lines, by means of, respectively *forehand and backhand chopped returns*, to the centre line near the Controller's baseline — 2

(g) *Sequences of Topspin-and-Backspin Strokes.* Play 15 double sequences of *forehand chop* and *backhand drive* against balls which have been respectively Driven to the Forehand and Pushed to Backhand — 3 (Total 30 balls)

(h) *Sequences of Topspin-and-Backspin Strokes.* Play the reverse of (g), (i.e. 'Backhand' for 'Forehand' and vice versa) — 3 (Total 30 balls)

(i) *Backhand Attack 'Distribution'.* Play 10 triple sequences thus: *Dropshot* to Area E; *Backhand drive* to Area F; *Backhand drive* to Area G; and repeat etc. Controller returns all balls to Area H. — 3

(j) *Loop-Topspin Forehand.* Candidate to demonstrate *loop drive* 5 times, by either bouncing the ball to his own convenience, or requesting chopped services of suitable length and strength, to suit his requirements. The aim is to show understanding of the 'loop' technique, and a continuity of loop drives is not demanded.

NOTE: For 'Penholder' styles, for 'Backhand' read: 'To the Left of the Body'

It must be appreciated that these regulations are subject to change from time to time. The latest Test paper is available from the English Table Tennis Association.

Everything you need to know for taking these tests is contained in this book and, with study and practice, there is no reason why you should not be capable of passing them all within a short period of time.

96